VEGAN*easy*

VEGAN*easy*

5 Delicious Food in Ingredients

Denise Smart

EBURY
PRESS

Contents

INTRODUCTION

This book is a celebration of veg and simplicity.

Vegan cooking isn't complicated, expensive or dull. You can make delicious food with just a few ingredients, often in less than 30 minutes, using everyday ingredients.

In this book, you will find over 60 quick-and-easy recipes for every mealtime, including snacks, divided into three chapters. We all love brunch and need quick, everyday breakfast ideas too, so both are covered in chapter 1 (page 21), with some make-ahead ideas in there as well. The mains chapter contains hearty and light dishes because you might want your main meal at lunchtime. There are also simple ideas for a packed lunch, really quick evening meals, and for something that looks and tastes special for when you've got people round – you'll find them all in chapter 2 (page 67). The final chapter is devoted to sweet things – puddings, desserts and sweet snacks (page 143).

Every recipe uses five ingredients – mostly fresh or perhaps a herb or spice to liven things up. On top of these, there are five 'basic' ingredients that recur throughout the book. They are inexpensive and essential cupboard items, so get these in your kitchen ahead of time and you will be ready to make fast, tasty, vegan meals any time of day.

The recipes will hopefully inspire you to go on and create recipes of your own. Whether you are a committed vegan or someone who wants to eat the occasional vegan meal, I hope you will find this book useful.

So let's get started…

HOW TO COOK
WITH 5 INGREDIENTS

You'll find these five basics used throughout this book in addition to the five ingredients listed in the recipes. You'll probably already have most of them to hand – they are ingredients that you only need to buy once in a while but will keep for weeks. If you have these staples stored in your fridge or cupboard the world is your oyster.

OLIVE OIL

A mild-flavoured olive oil is great for cooking and can also be used in salad dressings and for drizzling over foods. You could stock up on an extra virgin olive oil too, if you wanted, but it's not essential. Extra virgin olive oil adds excellent extra flavour to dressings and dishes, but don't use it for cooking.

RAPESEED OIL

Use this oil for shallow- or deep-frying. It can also be used in baking.

SALT AND BLACK PEPPER

Used throughout the book to season dishes to taste. Choose a good-quality sea salt and freshly ground black pepper.

VEGAN STOCK CUBES

Again, choose good-quality stock cubes. They are a clever way to pack more flavour into your cooking. Check labels as some vegetable stock cubes contain milk derivatives.

VEGAN MILK

You can usually find vegan plant milks in the chiller cabinet and on the shelves in shops. The non-chilled milks tend to be a bit cheaper, but taste exactly the same as the refrigerated ones. Keep a plant milk on hand in your cupboard or in the fridge. Choose unsweetened – check the label for sneaky additions. Fortified ones are a good source of calcium and vitamins B2, B12 and D. In general, they can be used interchangeably in cooking, so it is all down to the

flavour you prefer. In the book, you'll see recommendations for milks that work particularly well in recipes, but if you have another milk to hand, use that instead.

Soya milk
Made from soya beans, this has a very subtle flavour.

Almond (and other nuts) milk
Made by blending almonds with water. Good for cooking or pouring on cereals, it has a mild nutty flavour.

Coconut milk
Adds a tropical flavour. The taste is stronger than other milks and coconut milk typically has a higher fat content. Great as a drink in its own right.

HOW TO COOK WITH 5 INGREDIENTS

INGREDIENTS NOTES

BEANS AND PULSES

Cans of precooked beans and pulses in water are a great time-saver and a good source of protein and fibre. Kidney beans, black beans, green lentils and chickpeas are great ones to have in the cupboard. Save the liquid from cans of chickpeas to make meringues or to thicken sauces. Choose cans with no added salt.

CHOPPED TOMATOES

Add seasoned cans of tomatoes to recipes for an additional quick flavour boost – herb, garlic and chilli are all excellent.

FRUIT AND VEGETABLES

Eat a rainbow a day, shop regularly to avoid waste and choose seasonal and home-grown options (to reduce air miles) wherever you can – seasonal and local tend to be cheaper than imported fruit and veg too. Good basics to have are onions, potatoes, carrots and coloured peppers.

HERBS, SPICES AND PASTES

Instant flavour providers with minimal hassle – try customising the recipes here with harissa, Thai curry, Indian, jerk, chipotle, Moroccan, sundried tomato, olive tapenade and free-from pesto. If using pastes, remember to check the label to ensure they are vegan (some contain milk powder or fish sauce).

NUTS AND SEEDS

Perfect for adding crunch and texture and a good source of fatty acids, protein and fibre. Make your own nut butters using peanuts, cashews or almonds. Sprinkle a handful of seeds or nuts over your breakfast, soups or salads. Packs of mixed seeds make a great snack. Milled flaxseeds, mixed with water, can be added to cakes in place of eggs.

PASTA AND NOODLES

Most dried varieties of pasta are suitable for vegans, but there are now vegan varieties of fresh pasta and gnocchi too. Rice noodles and many other varieties of noodles are vegan-friendly, but check the label. You can also make your own vegetable noodles, such as with courgette, if you want to pack more veg in.

PASTRY

Save time with ready-made vegan shortcrust, puff or filo pastry, which are all readily available.

RICE AND GRAINS

I like to keep a selection of brown, jasmine, basmati, risotto and pudding rice in my kitchen. Not just an accompaniment, rice easily absorbs other flavours to make a delicious main in its own right. For grains, try buckwheat and quinoa (both technically seeds), couscous, spelt, barley and freekah. The packs of microwave grains and rice make a meal in minutes and are a good way of trying different grains.

SPREADS

There are many delicious vegan spreads to enjoy on your toast and to cook and bake with. Make sure, when baking, that you use a vegan spread that is marked suitable for baking, otherwise the recipe might not work.

TOFU

Bean curd, or tofu, is derived from soya. It is made by curdling fresh soya milk, pressing it into a solid block and then cooling it. An excellent source of protein, tofu is a versatile ingredient.

VEGAN YOGHURT

Vegan plant-based yoghurt is available in many varieties, but plain, vanilla and coconut are common ones. Eat with cereal, pancakes and puddings. Also great to stir into sauces for added richness. As with vegan milks, find your favourite.

INGREDIENTS NOTES

HANDY KITCHEN EQUIPMENT

PANS

You will need a medium to large frying pan or wok. Make sure the frying pan has a heatproof handle so that it can go from the hob to the oven or under the grill. You will also need good-quality saucepans with lids, good-sized non-stick baking trays, sheets and a roasting tin.

KNIVES

Make sure you have at least two good-quality sharp knives, a small one for paring and slicing and a larger one for chopping, plus a couple of chopping boards.

FOOD PROCESSOR

A food processor is brilliant for whizzing up pastes and pestos, blending soups and chopping vegetables and nuts. Mini choppers and stick blenders are cheaper and handier, but might not be quite as versatile.

EXTRAS

Mixing bowls, a colander or sieve, a grater and/or a microplane, spoons for stirring, slotted spoons, a vegetable peeler, balloon whisk and tongs will all speed up your cooking in the kitchen too.

MEASURING

A set of kitchen scales and measuring spoons, along with a measuring jug, are essential for accurate measuring of ingredients.

NUTRITIONAL NOTES

It is essential that we all eat a balanced diet. A vegan diet is a good way of ensuring that you eat your recommended five portions of fruit and vegetables, but you also need to make sure you eat a wide range of foods supplying protein, carbohydrates, fat (including omega-3 fatty acids), vitamins and minerals.

HOW MUCH DO I NEED?

This table shows the official Reference Intake (RI) figures; the figures are based on a moderately active adult, but remember your individual needs vary, so these figures should be used as a guide. RIs for total fat, sat. fat, sugar and salt are maximum daily amounts, so you should aim not to exceed these figures.

REFERENCE INTAKES (RI)	WOMEN	MEN
Energy (Kcal)	2,000	2,500
Fat (g)	70	95
Saturates (g)	20	30
Carbohydrates (g)	260	300
Sugars (g)	90	120
Protein (g)	50	55
Salt (g)	6	6

For nutrients that are more commonly found in meat and dairy, here are some good vegan sources...

VEGAN SOURCES OF PROTEIN
(Daily recommended amount is 50g for women and 55g for men)

Soya products, such as tofu, soya milk and yoghurt
Nuts and seeds
Pseudo-grains, including quinoa and buckwheat
Beans
Lentils
Grains, including spelt and freekeh

VEGAN SOURCES OF IRON
(Daily recommended amount is 14.8mg for women and 8.7mg for men)

Soya products, such as tofu, soya milk and yoghurt
Lentils, beans and peas
Nuts and seeds
Dried fruit, including apricots
Leafy greens
Dark chocolate
Wholegrains

VEGAN SOURCES OF B12
(Daily recommended amount for adults is 1.5mcg)

Nutritional yeast
Yeast extract
Fortified vegan milks, yoghurt and cereals

VEGAN SOURCES OF VITAMIN C
(Daily recommended amount for adults is 40mg)

Citrus fruits
Peppers
Broccoli
Leafy greens
Cauliflower
Tomatoes

VEGAN SOURCES OF OMEGA-3
(No recommended amount. With a vegan diet, aim to eat 1 tbsp of chia seeds or ground flaxseeds or 6 walnut halves daily)

Chia seeds, flaxseeds, hemp seeds
Walnuts
Seaweed
Soya products, such as tofu, soya milk and yoghurt
Leafy greens

VEGAN SOURCES OF CALCIUM
(Daily recommended amount for adults is 700mg)

Almonds
Sesame seeds and tahini
Leafy greens
Fortified soya products, such as tofu, soya milk and yoghurt
Broccoli

NUTRITIONAL NOTES

Breakfast & Brunch

Find hearty and healthy breakfast ideas here – pancakes, porridge, pastries and even a vegan twist on a classic British fry-up, as well as fruity smoothies, breakfast bowls and nutty bars to eat on the go.

Enjoy the first meal of the day in style...

What would you like?

Breakfast & Brunch

Spiced scrambled tofu

Garlicky mushrooms
on toasted farls

Fruit & nut granola

Smoky sweet potato
& beetroot hash

Hearty porridge

Apricot & pistachio pastries
with cinnamon sugar

Griddled avocados
with crispy pitta chips

Chocolate hazelnut spread

Quick breakfast smoothies

Coconut & mango quinoa bowl

Easy pancakes

Date, peanut & almond breakfast bars

Tomato-stuffed portabella mushrooms on toast

Banana bread

One-pan brunch bake

Smoky beans on toast

SPICED SCRAMBLED TOFU

Add whatever veggies you like to this tasty tofu – mushrooms are a great addition. Serve on toast, if you like.

Serves 2 | Ready in 10 minutes

200g firm tofu, smoked works well

1 small red onion, thinly sliced

2 tsp mild or medium curry powder

2 tomatoes, chopped

100g spinach, roughly chopped

BASICS
rapeseed oil, salt and black pepper

Dry the tofu on kitchen paper and break it into bite-sized pieces.

Heat 1 tablespoon of rapeseed oil in a frying pan, add the onion and cook over a medium heat for 2 to 3 minutes, until starting to soften. Stir in the curry powder and cook for 1 minute, then add the tomatoes.

Add a little more oil if necessary, then add the tofu and cook over a medium heat for 3 to 4 minutes or until starting to turn golden, then gently stir. Cook until the tofu is golden on all sides.

Stir in the spinach and cook until just wilted.

Season with salt and black pepper. Divide between two plates and serve immediately.

NUTRITION
Kcal 258 | fat 18g | sat. fat 2g | carbs 7g | sugars 5g | fibre 3g | protein 15g | salt 0.98g

GARLICKY MUSHROOMS ON TOASTED FARLS

Simple to make – you could add a couple of tablespoons of vegan yoghurt for extra richness. If you can't find farls, serve on toasted sourdough.

Serves 2 | Ready in 10 minutes

300g mixed mushrooms, such as chestnut, portabella and button, sliced

2 garlic cloves, crushed

1 tbsp lemon juice

2 tbsp chopped flat-leaf parsley

4 potato farls, toasted

BASICS
olive oil, salt and black pepper

Heat 1 tablespoon of olive oil in a medium frying pan over a high heat. Reduce the heat slightly. Add the mushrooms and fry for 6 minutes, stirring occasionally, until the mushrooms are golden.

Stir in the garlic and cook for 1 minute. Add the lemon juice and season to taste with salt and black pepper.

Remove from the heat and stir in the parsley, then divide the mushrooms among the potato farls.

NUTRITION
Kcal 315 | fat 10g | sat. fat 1g | carbs 47g | sugars 5g | fibre 5g | protein 7g | salt 1.22g

FRUIT & NUT GRANOLA

Homemade granola is simple to make. Store any leftover granola in an airtight container and it will last for up to 2 weeks. Serve with your favourite vegan milk or yoghurt.

Makes 8 portions | Ready in 30 minutes

6 tbsp maple syrup

250g porridge oats

100g pecans, chopped

100g mixed seeds, such as sunflower, pumpkin and flaxseeds

100g dried mixed berries, such as blueberries, cranberries and cherries

BASICS
rapeseed oil

Heat the oven to 150°C/130°C fan/300°F/Gas mark 2. Gently warm the maple syrup and 2 tablespoons of rapeseed oil in a small saucepan on the hob.

Put the oats, nuts and seeds in a large bowl and mix well. Pour over the warm maple mixture and stir so everything is evenly coated.

Spread over a large, non-stick baking tray and cook in the oven for 20 to 25 minutes or until golden, stirring once after about 10 minutes.

Remove from the oven and allow to cool, then stir in the berries before serving warm or cold.

NUTRITION (EXCLUDING MILK/YOGHURT)
Kcal 383 | fat 20g | sat. fat 2g | carbs 39g | sugars 16g | fibre 5g | protein 8g | salt 0.05g

SMOKY SWEET POTATO & BEETROOT HASH

A hearty start to the day and packed full of healthy nutrients. Fresh beetroot adds a wonderful colour.

Serves 2 | Ready in 30 minutes

400g sweet potatoes, peeled and cut into 2cm cubes

250g raw beetroot, skins scrubbed and ends trimmed, cut into 2cm cubes

125g chopped kale

1 red onion, sliced

1 tsp smoked paprika (or regular paprika, if you prefer)

BASICS
rapeseed oil, salt and black pepper

Put the sweet potato in one half of the steamer and the beetroot in the other half. Cover and steam for 7 minutes. If you don't have a steamer, put the sweet potato then the beetroot in a microwavable bowl, cover each with 2 tablespoons tap water, cover with cling film and cook for about 3 to 4 minutes or until tender. Stir in the kale and allow to wilt.

Add the kale and steam for a further 3 minutes, until tender.

Heat 2 tablespoons of rapeseed oil in a frying pan, add the onion and cook over a medium heat for 3 to 4 minutes until softened.

Stir in the sweet potato, beetroot and kale. Fry over a medium heat for 7 to 8 minutes, turning occasionally until browned. Stir in the paprika and season to taste with salt and black pepper. Cook for a further minute.

Divide between two plates and serve immediately.

NUTRITION
Kcal 401 | fat 13g | sat. fat 1g | carbs 56g | sugars 24g | fibre 14g | protein 8g | salt 0.55g

HEARTY PORRIDGE

Customise this recipe to suit your taste – peanut butter works well served with jam, use soya milk instead of almond, or top with other fresh fruit, such as blackberries, apple, kiwi, strawberries or raspberries.

Serves 2 | Ready in 10 minutes

75g porridge oats

1–2 tbsp almond butter

1 banana, sliced

handful mixed seeds

2 tbsp date nectar or maple syrup

BASICS
vegan milk (almond works well)

Put the oats, 300ml of vegan milk and 150ml of tap water in a pan. Bring to the boil, then reduce the heat to low and cook for 3 to 4 minutes, stirring to prevent the oats sticking to the bottom of the pan.

When the oats are tender, stir in the almond butter to taste.

Divide between two bowls and top with the sliced banana, seeds and date nectar or maple syrup.

NUTRITION
Kcal 335 | fat 12g | sat. fat 1g | carbs 46g | sugars 18g | fibre 5g | protein 9g | salt 0.2g

BREAKFAST & BRUNCH

APRICOT & PISTACHIO PASTRIES WITH CINNAMON SUGAR

Store any remaining pastries in an airtight container; they will keep for 2 to 3 days.

Makes 12 | Ready in 30 minutes

320–375g pack ready-rolled
vegan puff pastry

6 tbsp apricot jam

100g pistachio kernels, chopped

2 tsp caster sugar

½ tsp ground cinnamon

BASICS
vegan milk

Heat the oven to 220°C/200°C fan/425°F/Gas mark 7. Line a baking tray with baking paper.

Unroll the pastry sheet, keeping it on the baking paper. Spread with the apricot jam, then sprinkle with the pistachios.

Roll up both sides from the longest sides, until they meet in the centre.

Using a sharp knife, cut into 2cm-thick slices. In a small bowl, mix together the sugar and cinnamon.

Brush some vegan milk over the pastries, then roll the sides in the cinnamon sugar. Place, cut-side up, on the baking tray and sprinkle the remaining cinnamon sugar over the top. Chill for 10 minutes.

Bake for 13 to 15 minutes until risen, golden and crisp.

Serve whilst still warm.

NUTRITION (PER PASTRY)
Kcal 177 | fat 11g | sat. fat 4g | carbs 16g | sugars 7g | fibre 2g | protein 3g | salt 0.2g

GRIDDLED AVOCADOS WITH CRISPY PITTA CHIPS

Griddling or barbecuing the avocado adds a lovely smokiness. Kidney beans also work well here instead of black beans, if you prefer them.

Serves 2 | Ready in 15 minutes

2 pitta breads

1 large avocado, ripe but firm

1 lime, halved

100g canned black beans

4 tbsp tomato salsa

BASICS
olive oil, salt and black pepper

Heat the oven to 180°C/160°C fan/350°F/Gas mark 4. Open the pitta breads, to make two halves, and cut into bite- sized strips. Place on a baking tray and brush both sides with a little olive oil and season, then bake for 8 to 10 minutes until crisp and golden, turning halfway through.

Meanwhile, halve the avocado and remove the stone. Brush the flesh with a little olive oil and season.

Heat a griddle pan over a medium heat and add the avocado, flesh-side down. Don't move the avocado halves and cook for 2–3 minutes until the avocado releases itself from the pan and has nice griddle marks. Add the lime halves to the pan for the last minute to char.

Meanwhile, warm the beans according to the pack instructions, then drain and squeeze over the juice from one half of the lime.

Put the avocado onto a plate and squeeze over the juice of the remaining lime half. Spoon over the beans and salsa. Serve with the pitta chips.

NUTRITION
Kcal 496 | fat 24g | sat. fat 5g | carbs 51g | sugars 5g | fibre 9g | protein 14g | salt 0.92g

CHOCOLATE HAZELNUT SPREAD

It's so easy to make your own chocolate spread with wholesome ingredients. Delicious served spread on hot toast or waffles. It will keep for 3 weeks in the fridge.

Makes a 250g jar | Ready in 15 minutes

200g blanched hazelnuts

3 tbsp cacao or cocoa powder

2 tbsp maple syrup

1 tsp vanilla extract

your favourite bread, toasted

Heat the oven to 180°C/160°C fan/350°F/Gas mark 4. Put the hazelnuts on a baking tray and cook for about 8 to 10 minutes until toasted, then cool slightly.

Put the nuts in a food processor and blend until they turn to nut butter, scraping down the sides from time to time – this will take about 5 minutes. Add the cacao or cocoa and process until combined and smooth.

Add the maple syrup and vanilla extract and blend again, then add 2–3 tablespoons of cold water to loosen the spread slightly.

Transfer to a jar and serve spread on toast.

NUTRITION (PER TBSP)
Kcal 78 | fat 7g | sat. fat 1g | carbs 2g | sugars 2g | fibre 1g | protein 2g | salt 0.01g

QUICK BREAKFAST SMOOTHIES

These delicious fruit and veg smoothies make a filling start to the day.

Each serves 2 | Ready in 5 minutes

MANGO, BANANA, GINGER & COCONUT

200g fresh or frozen chopped mango flesh

1 banana, chopped

2.5cm piece fresh ginger, peeled and finely chopped

100ml coconut water

100g vegan yoghurt (coconut is good)

AVOCADO, APPLE, SPINACH, LIME & MINT

1 avocado, peeled, stoned and chopped

200ml apple juice

50g fresh spinach or kale

juice 1 lime

small handful mint

BERRIES, BANANA, OATS & NUTS

150g fresh or frozen mixed berries

1 small banana, chopped

200g vegan yoghurt (vanilla is good)

2 tbsp porridge oats

small handful nuts (about 10), such as cashews or almonds

Put all the ingredients in a blender or food processor and blitz until smooth. Add a little more water, juice or yoghurt for the desired consistency.

Pour into glasses or small bowls and chill in the fridge. These are best drunk the day they are made, but will keep in the fridge for up to 1 day.

MANGO, BANANA, GINGER & COCONUT
Kcal 203 | fat 10g | sat. fat 9g | carbs 24g | sugars 21g | fibre 3g | protein 3g | salt 0.14g

AVOCADO, APPLE, SPINACH, LIME & MINT
Kcal 238 | fat 19g | sat. fat 4g | carbs 11g | sugars 10g | fibre 5g | protein 3g | salt 0.04g

BERRIES, BANANA, OATS & NUTS
Kcal 246 | fat 8g | sat. fat 1g | carbs 32g | sugars 20g | fibre 5g | protein 8g | salt 0.07g

BREAKFAST & BRUNCH

COCONUT & MANGO QUINOA BOWL

Prepare the night before, leave in the fridge and you will have a brilliant breakfast ready to go, to power you through the day. Make in jars, then you can take it to work.

Serves 2 | Ready in 5 minutes, plus 2 hours or overnight chilling time

250g cooked quinoa

2 tbsp mixed seeds

200g fresh mango chunks,
   halved if large

50g coconut flakes

2 passion fruit

BASICS
vegan milk

Put the quinoa, 400ml of vegan milk, the seeds and most of the mango and coconut flakes, reserving a little of both for serving, in a large bowl.

Stir to mix everything together. Cover and place in the fridge for a couple of hours or overnight, so the quinoa absorbs the liquid.

Stir before serving and add a little extra milk if a runnier consistency is preferred.

Divide between two bowls, then scoop out the seeds and pulp from the passion fruit and drizzle over the quinoa.

Top with the reserved mango and sprinkle over the coconut flakes.

NUTRITION
Kcal 510 | fat 27g | sat. fat 17g | carbs 48g | sugars 22g | fibre 11g | protein 12g | salt 0.77g

EASY PANCAKES

These pancakes work particularly well with the buckwheat, which is a good source of protein. You could add 1 mashed banana to the batter.

Makes 12 pancakes | Ready in 15 minutes

75g buckwheat or plain flour

1 tsp baking powder

1 tbsp maple syrup, plus extra for drizzling

125g blueberries or 1 small grated eating apple

vanilla-flavoured vegan yoghurt

BASICS
salt, vegan milk, rapeseed oil

Put the flour and baking powder in a mixing bowl with a pinch of salt and stir well. In a jug, beat together 160ml of vegan milk, 1 tablespoon of rapeseed oil and the maple syrup.

Gradually pour this into the flour mixture, mixing until you have a smooth batter. Fold in half the blueberries or all the grated apple.

Heat a large frying pan, add a little rapeseed oil and wipe over the pan with kitchen paper. When hot, drop in heaped tablespoons of the batter and cook over a medium heat for about 2 minutes or until bubbles start to appear on the surface, then flip over and cook for a further 30 seconds to 1 minute until cooked.

Remove to a plate and keep warm, then repeat with the remaining batter.

Serve the pancakes with a dollop of yoghurt, the reserved blueberries (if using) and a drizzle of maple syrup.

NUTRITION (PER PANCAKE, EXCLUDING YOGHURT)
Kcal 43 | fat 1g | sat. fat 0.1g | carbs 6g | sugars 2g | fibre 1g | protein 1g | salt 0.2g

BREAKFAST & BRUNCH

DATE, PEANUT & ALMOND BREAKFAST BARS

These chewy fruit-and-nut bars are perfect for an on-the-go breakfast or snacking. They will keep for up to a week in an airtight container.

Makes 12 bars | Ready in 20 minutes, plus 1 hour or overnight chilling

200g pitted dates, chopped

2 tbsp date nectar or maple syrup

75g peanut butter

200g porridge oats

100g almonds, roughly chopped

Line a 20cm square tin with baking paper.

Put the dates, date nectar or maple syrup, peanut butter and 4 tablespoons of tap/cold water in a small pan and heat gently, stirring, until the mixture is combined and melted.

Pour into a food processor and pulse until the dates are broken up, then add the oats and nuts and pulse until the mixture is combined.

Spoon into the lined tin and press down with the back of a spoon. Cover and chill in the fridge for about 1 hour or overnight, then cut into 12 bars.

NUTRITION (PER BAR)
Kcal 216 | fat 9g | sat. fat 1g | carbs 25g | sugars 13g | fibre 3g | protein 6g | salt 0.1g

TOMATO-STUFFED PORTABELLA MUSHROOMS ON TOAST

Quick to prepare and big on flavour. Serve on your favourite toasted bread.

Serves 2 | Ready in 25 minutes

4 large portabella mushrooms, stalks removed

2 sundried or sun-blushed tomatoes in oil, from a jar, chopped, plus 2 tbsp of the oil

16 cherry tomatoes

2 slices wholemeal toast

handful basil leaves

BASICS
salt and black pepper

Heat the oven to 200°C/180°C fan/400°F/Gas mark 6.

Place the mushrooms, open-side up, on a baking tray. Divide the sundried or sun-blushed tomatoes among the mushrooms, then add four cherry tomatoes to each. Season well with salt and black pepper.

Drizzle with the oil from the jar.

Roast for 15 to 20 minutes until tender, then serve two mushrooms per person on a slice of toast, garnished with basil leaves.

NUTRITION
Kcal 261 | fat 13g | sat. fat 2g | carbs 23g | sugars 11g | fibre 7g | protein 9g | salt 0.38g

BANANA BREAD

Delicious served toasted, this bread tastes even better the next day. Make variations of the bread by adding 50g chopped nuts or raisins.

Makes a 900g loaf/10 slices | Ready in 1 hour

3 ripe bananas, peeled

125g soft brown sugar

225g self-raising flour

1 tsp baking powder

2 tsp ground mixed spice

BASICS
rapeseed oil

Heat the oven to 180°C/160°C fan/350°F/Gas mark 4. Lightly oil a 900g loaf tin and line the base with baking paper.

Break the bananas into pieces, place in a large bowl and mash to a pulp. Pour in 5 tablespoons of rapeseed oil and the sugar and mix until combined. Stir in the flour, baking powder and mixed spice, then pour into the prepared tin.

Bake in the oven for 35 to 40 minutes, covering the top with foil if it becomes too brown, or until a skewer inserted into the centre comes out clean.

Allow to cool in the tin for 10 minutes, then transfer to a wire rack. Delicious served in thick slices warm or cold.

NUTRITION (PER SLICE)
Kcal 197 | fat 6g | sat. fat 0.5g | carbs 33g | sugars 15g | fibre 1g | protein 2g | salt 0.34g

BREAKFAST & BRUNCH

ONE-PAN BRUNCH BAKE

Perfect for a lazy morning and only one tray to wash up!

Serves 2 | Ready in 30 minutes

250g frozen oven-bake potato
 wedges

4 vegan sausages

6 mini portabellini mushrooms

2 tomatoes, halved

400g can baked beans or smoky
 beans (see page 64)

BASICS
salt and black pepper,
 rapeseed oil

Heat the oven to 200°C/180°C fan/400°F/Gas mark 6. Spread out the potato wedges in a non-stick roasting tin or baking tray and cook for 10 minutes.

Add the sausages and mushrooms. Season, drizzle with 1 tablespoon of rapeseed oil and gently toss together. Return to the oven and cook for a further 15 minutes, turning the sausages and wedges and adding the tomatoes halfway through the cooking time. Cook until the potatoes are crispy and tomatoes softened.

Meanwhile, warm the baked/smoky beans in a pan or microwave.

Divide the mixture between two plates and serve with the warm baked beans.

NUTRITION
Kcal 547 | fat 14g | sat. fat 3g | carbs 66g | sugars 16g | fibre 18g | protein 29g | salt 2.14g

SMOKY BEANS ON TOAST

Perfect served simply on toast or as an accompaniment.

Serve 2 | Ready in 10 minutes

**400g can cannellini beans,
  drained and rinsed**

200g passata

2 tbsp soft brown sugar

2 tsp smoked paprika

4 slices sourdough

BASICS
salt and black pepper

Place all the ingredients apart from the bread in a pan, bring to the boil, reduce the heat, then cover and simmer for 5 minutes or until the beans are tender. Season to taste with salt and black pepper.

Meanwhile, toast the sourdough and serve the smoky beans on top.

NUTRITION
Kcal 400 | fat 2g | sat. fat 1g | carbs 76g | sugars 27g | fibre 6g | protein 16g | salt 1.7g

BREAKFAST & BRUNCH

Mains

There are recipes for light and larger meals here, whatever your appetite or the occasion: Try *Pea & Fresh Mint Falafel* for a light bite or *One-pot Cajun Rice & Beans* when you're really hungry. Recipes that are great for lunchboxes include *Harissa-roasted Squash & Freekeh Salad* and *Tandoori Tofu Wraps*. There are dishes special enough to serve to family and friends, such as *Asparagus, Basil & Lemon Risotto* and *Griddled Peach & Almond Salad*, and fun ideas for weeknights, such as *Shiitake Mushroom Ramen* and *Katsu Aubergine Curry*.

What would you like?

Mains

Teriyaki tofu stir-fry

Pizzas

Tandoori tofu wraps

Miso-glazed aubergines
& sticky rice

Chipotle sweet potato
& black bean curry

Pea & fresh mint falafel

One-pot Cajun rice & beans

Za'atar roasted cauliflower

Chipotle bean burgers

Mediterranean veg
& chickpea tagine

Katsu aubergine curry

Jerk cauliflower steaks,
rice & beans

Tortilla bowls

Shiitake mushroom ramen

One pan mushroom &
spinach pie

Harissa-roasted squash
& freekeh salad

Falafel, carrot & grains bowl

Thai red pumpkin curry

Summer olive tart

Warming lentil pie

Asparagus, basil
& lemon risotto

Sweet potato gnocchi
with sage

Pasta three ways

Taste of the sea tofu & chips

Leek & potato pie

Rice noodle chilli stir-fry

Griddled peach
  & almond salad

New potato & fennel bake

Chermoula-spiced broccoli
  fritters

TERIYAKI TOFU STIR-FRY

A quick-and-easy midweek meal – tofu and vegetables coated in a delicious sticky sauce. Serve with noodles, if you prefer.

Serves 2 | Ready in 20 minutes

200g firm tofu

3 tbsp teriyaki sauce

1 red pepper, deseeded and cut into thin strips

4 spring onions, cut into thin strips

250g pouch long-grain or basmati rice

BASICS
rapeseed oil

Place the tofu between two pieces of kitchen paper and put a chopping board or heavy weight on top. Leave for at least 10 minutes, to remove excess water, then cut into bite-sized cubes.

Put the cubes in a bowl and gently stir in 1 tablespoon of the teriyaki sauce until the tofu is coated.

Heat 1 tablespoon of rapeseed oil in a wok or frying pan over a high heat and add the tofu. Reduce the heat slightly and cook for 3 to 4 minutes, turning occasionally, until lightly browned on all sides.

Add the pepper and most of the spring onions, reserving a few for garnish. Cook for 2 to 3 minutes until softened, then stir in the remaining teriyaki sauce. Stir to coat, then remove from the heat.

Meanwhile, cook the rice according to the packet instructions. Divide between two plates and serve the stir-fry on top, garnished with the reserved spring onions.

NUTRITION
Kcal 433 | fat 17g | sat. fat 2g | carbs 46g | sugars 7g | fibre 5g | protein 22g | salt 2.51g

PIZZAS

It is really easy to make your own pizzas. Just follow the recipe, then top with pizza sauce and your favourite toppings to customise. If you are short of time, you could use a ready-made pizza base.

Makes 1 x 20cm pizza | Ready in 30 minutes, plus 15 minutes rising

145g pizza base mix

BASICS
olive oil

Put the pizza base mix in a bowl and make a well in the centre. Using a wooden spoon, stir in 100ml of lukewarm water to form a dough.

Put the dough on a lightly floured surface and knead for 5 minutes until smooth and elastic.

Heat the oven to 220°C/200°C fan/425°F/Gas mark 7. Lightly oil a baking sheet. Place the dough on the baking sheet and using a rolling pin, roll out to a 20–21cm circle, (the oil on the baking sheet helps the dough to stick, making it easier to roll). Leave to rise in a warm place for 15 minutes.

Spread with the sauce of your choice, then the toppings.

Bake for 10 to 15 minutes until the dough is crisp and golden. Serve drizzled with extra olive oil.

PIZZAS toppings

HAWAIIAN

Spread the base of the pizza with 4 tbsp barbecue sauce, chop 2 rings of pineapple from a can, add to the pizza with 1 deseeded and chopped red pepper (or you could chop up 2 slices vegan ham). Sprinkle over 50g grated vegan mozzarella and bake.

Kcal 678 | fat 15g | sat. fat 11g | carbs 115g | sugars 37g | fibre 10g | protein 15g | salt 2.4g

ARTICHOKE & ROASTED PEPPER

Spread the base of the pizza with 4 tbsp sundried tomato paste, scatter over 6 halved chargrilled artichokes and some slices of roasted red pepper from jars. Bake, then scatter over some rocket leaves or basil when the pizza comes out of the oven.

Kcal 763 | fat 34g | sat. fat 3g | carbs 85g | sugars 9g | fibre 13g | protein 22g | salt 6.73g

MARGHERITA

Spread the base of the pizza with 4 tbsp bought pizza sauce. Arrange tomatoes over the top (I used 1 sliced tomato and 4 halved cherry tomatoes) and 50g grated vegan mozzarella. Bake, then scatter over a large handful of basil leaves when the pizza comes out of the oven.

Kcal 607 | fat 16g | sat. fat 12g | carbs 94g | sugars 14g | fibre 9g | protein 17g | salt 1.9g

MAINS

CARAMELISED ONION

Spread the base of the pizza with 4 tbsp bought pizza sauce. Heat 1 tablespoon olive oil in a frying pan and cook 2 sliced red onions over a low heat with 1 teaspoon sugar for about 10 minutes until caramelised. Season well and spoon over the pizza. Sprinkle over 50g grated vegan mozzarella and bake.

Kcal 767 | fat 27g | sat. fat 13g | carbs 109g | sugars 25g | fibre 11g | protein 17g | salt 1.9g

MIDDLE EASTERN BUTTERNUT SQUASH & POMEGRANATE

Drizzle 250g cubed butternut squash with a little olive oil. Season well and cook in the hot oven for 20 minutes until softened. Spread the pizza base with hummus or bought pizza sauce, then top with the butternut squash. Bake, then scatter over 25g pomegranate seeds and a large handful of rocket leaves when the pizza comes out of the oven.

Kcal 700 | fat 24g | sat. fat 2g | carbs 94g | sugars 16g | fibre 13g | protein 21g | salt 1.1g

TANDOORI TOFU WRAPS

These kebabs taste better if left to marinate. You can also use the marinade to coat vegetables, such as aubergines and courgettes. Cook on the barbecue or under the grill.

Serves 2 | Ready in 1 hour 30 minutes

400g firm tofu

100g coconut yoghurt, plus extra to serve

2 tbsp tandoori masala spice mix

2 unwaxed lemons

4 Indian-style breads, such as chapatis or roti

BASICS
rapeseed oil, salt and black pepper

Place the tofu between two pieces of kitchen paper and put a chopping board or heavy weight on top. Leave for at least 10 minutes, to remove excess water, then cut into 16 cubes.

Mix together the yoghurt, spice mix, 1 tablespoon of rapeseed oil and the finely grated zest and juice of one of the lemons in a large bowl, season and stir in the tofu. Leave to marinate for 1 hour, if time allows.

Thread the tofu onto four soaked wooden skewers, allowing four pieces per skewer, or two long metal skewers.

Brush a griddle pan or barbecue with a little oil. When hot, add the skewers and cook for about 5 minutes on each side, brushing with any remaining marinade, until lightly charred. Cut the remaining lemon in half and griddle for a few minutes until charred.

Spread the base of the breads with the extra yoghurt, put the tofu on top and drizzle with juice from the squeezed charred lemon halves. Serve immediately.

NUTRITION
Kcal 705| fat 35g | sat. fat 11g | carbs 53g | sugars 3g | fibre 5g | protein 43g | salt 0.7g

MISO-GLAZED AUBERGINES & STICKY RICE

Miso and aubergine combined is a match made in heaven. This Japanese recipe is perfect for cooking on the BBQ.

Serves 2 | Ready in 50 minutes

3 tbsp rice wine vinegar or mirin

¼ cucumber, halved lengthways, seeds removed and cut into half-moon shapes

2 aubergines

3 tbsp white miso paste

100g Thai sticky rice

BASICS
salt, rapeseed oil

Place 2 tablespoons of the rice wine and a pinch of salt in a bowl and stir to dissolve. Add the cucumber and mix well. Place a heavy weight on top and leave to one side.

Heat the grill to high. Line a baking tray with foil. Cut the aubergines in half lengthways, then score the flesh into diamond shapes, being careful not to cut all the way through.

In a small bowl, mix together the miso paste, remaining rice wine vinegar or mirin and 1 tablespoon of cold water.

Place the aubergines, cut-side up, on the lined baking tray and brush the flesh with a little rapeseed oil. Place under the grill and cook for 15 minutes until softened.

Brush with half the miso glaze and cook for another 10 to 15 minutes until golden and the flesh is very soft, brushing halfway through with the remaining glaze.

Meanwhile, cook the rice according to the pack instructions. Serve the rice in bowls and add the aubergines. Drain the cucumber from the liquid and serve alongside.

NUTRITION
Kcal 414 | fat 9g | sat. fat 1g | carbs 68g | sugars 15g | fibre 10g | protein 10g | salt 2.09g

CHIPOTLE SWEET POTATO & BLACK BEAN CURRY

Who doesn't love a chilli on a cold winter's night? This one is smoky and delicious. Serve with rice or tortillas.

Serves 2 | Ready in 45 minutes

1 large sweet potato (about 250g), peeled and cut into small chunks

2 tsp chipotle paste, or to taste

400g can chopped tomatoes with onion and garlic

400g can black beans, drained and rinsed

75g long-grain rice

BASICS
rapeseed oil, vegan stock cube, salt and black pepper

Heat 1 tablespoon of rapeseed oil in a large saucepan and cook the sweet potato over a medium heat for 2 to 3 minutes, then stir in the chipotle paste, chopped tomatoes, 300ml of vegan stock and the beans.

Bring to the boil, cover and simmer over a gentle heat for 20 to 25 minutes, until the vegetables are tender. Season to taste with salt and black pepper.

Meanwhile, cook the rice in boiling salted water, following the pack instructions. Drain and divide between two bowls, then top with the chilli.

NUTRITION
Kcal 417 | fat 7g | sat. fat 1g | carbs 66g | sugars 15g | fibre 16g | protein 14g | salt 0.4g

PEA & FRESH MINT FALAFEL

These falafel are baked rather than deep-fried. They make a great lunch box addition, served with tomatoes and salad leaves in wraps.

Makes 16 falafel | Ready in 30 minutes, plus 30 minutes chilling

250g frozen peas

400g can chickpeas, drained well and rinsed

2–3 tsp harissa paste

4 tbsp chopped mint

100g plain vegan yoghurt

BASICS

salt and black pepper, rapeseed oil

Place the peas in a heatproof bowl and pour over some boiling water. Leave to stand for 2 to 3 minutes to defrost, then drain well. Place the chickpeas, peas, harissa paste and 2 tablespoons of the mint in a food processor and season well with salt and black pepper. Pulse until well combined.

Divide the chickpea mixture into 16 and roll into balls, then flatten slightly. Cover and chill in the fridge for 30 minutes.

Heat the oven to 190°C/170°C fan/375°F/Gas mark 5. Brush a large baking tray with a little rapeseed oil.

Place the falafel on the baking tray and bake for 15 minutes until crisp.

Meanwhile, place the yoghurt in a small bowl, add the remaining mint and season to taste. Serve the falafel with the yoghurt dip.

NUTRITION (PER FALAFEL WITH DIP)
Kcal 37 | fat 1g | sat. fat 0.1g | carbs 4g | sugars 1g | fibre 2g | protein 2g | salt 0.03g

ONE-POT CAJUN RICE & BEANS

This lightly spiced Cajun rice dish originated in Louisiana in the USA. It is easy to make as it is cooked all in one pan. You could replace the parsnip with carrot or 125g mushrooms.

Serves 2 | Ready in 25 minutes

1 parsnip, peeled and cut into bite-sized pieces

1 tbsp Cajun spice mix

125g easy-cook long-grain rice

400g can mixed bean salad with corn, drained and rinsed

400g can chopped tomatoes with onion and garlic

BASICS
rapeseed oil, vegan stock cube, salt and black pepper

Heat 1 tablespoon of rapeseed oil in a large sauté pan or saucepan, with a lid. Add the parsnip and spice and cook for 2 to 3 minutes. Stir in the rice to coat in the spice.

Stir in the beans, 300ml of vegan stock and the tomatoes. Cover and simmer for 20 minutes, stirring occasionally, until the rice is tender and most of the liquid has been absorbed. Season to taste with salt and black pepper.

Divide between two bowls and serve immediately.

NUTRITION
Kcal 431 | fat 8g | sat. fat 1g | carbs 74g | sugars 17g | fibre 11g | protein 11g | salt 0.53g

ZA'ATAR ROASTED CAULIFLOWER

Za'atar is a Middle Eastern blend of dried thyme, oregano, marjoram, sumac, toasted sesame seeds and salt. Any leftover cauliflower can be served in a salad or in a wrap.

Serves 4 | Ready in 1 hour

2 tbsp za'atar

1 whole cauliflower, leaves removed

1 large unwaxed lemon, halved

4 tbsp tahini

2 x 250g pouches mixed grains with lentils

BASICS
olive oil, salt and black pepper

Heat the oven to 200°C/180°C fan/400°F/Gas mark 6. In a large bowl, mix the za'atar with 3 tablespoons of olive oil and season. Add the cauliflower and turn to coat.

Put the cauliflower in a roasting tin and brush over any remaining spice mix. Roast for 40 to 45 minutes or until tender.

Squeeze one half of the lemon into a bowl, add the tahini, 4 tablespoons of cold water and some salt and whisk together until smooth and creamy.

Heat the grains according to the pack instructions and then divide between two bowls. Slice the cauliflower and serve on top of the grains, drizzled with the tahini sauce and a squeeze of lemon.

NUTRITION
Kcal 454 | fat 23g | sat. fat 4g | carbs 42g | sugars 4g | fibre 9g | protein 13g | salt 0.1g

CHIPOTLE BEAN BURGERS

So simple to make and packed full of smoky, spicy flavours. For a milder taste, just add 1 teaspoon of paste to the burgers.

Serves 2 | Ready in 15 minutes

400g can kidney beans, drained
  and rinsed

3 tsp chipotle paste

2 tbsp vegan mayonnaise

2 bread rolls, halved

handful mixed salad leaves

BASICS
salt and black pepper,
  rapeseed oil

Put the kidney beans, 2 teaspoons of the chipotle paste and a good sprinkling of salt and black pepper in a food processor and pulse until the mixture is roughly combined.

Shape the mixture into two burgers, then brush each with a little rapeseed oil.

Place under a preheated medium-hot grill or on a griddle pan or barbecue. Cook for 3 to 4 minutes on each side.

Meanwhile, mix the mayonnaise with the remaining teaspoon of chipotle paste.

Grill or griddle the rolls until lightly toasted, then put some salad leaves on the bases. Add the burgers and serve topped with the chipotle mayonnaise and roll tops.

NUTRITION
Kcal 454 | fat 22g | sat. fat 2g | carbs 44g | sugars 4g | fibre 12g | protein 13g | salt 0.98g

MAINS

MEDITERRANEAN VEG & CHICKPEA TAGINE

Remember to keep the drained chickpea water – it makes a great thickener and replaces egg white in meringues.

Serves 2 | Ready in 40 minutes

400g mixed Mediterranean vegetables (fresh or frozen), to contain onions, peppers, courgettes, aubergine, etc.

1 tbsp Moroccan spice mix

400g can chickpeas, drained and rinsed

400g can chopped tomatoes

110g pouch lemon-flavoured couscous

BASICS
rapeseed oil, vegan stock cube

Heat 1 tablespoon of rapeseed oil in a large wok or pan, add the vegetables and cook for 3 to 4 minutes. Add the spice mix and cook for 2 minutes.

Stir in the chickpeas, chopped tomatoes and 150ml of vegan stock, then cover and simmer for 30 minutes, stirring occasionally, until the sauce has thickened and the vegetables are tender.

Meanwhile, cook the couscous according to the pack instructions.

Divide the couscous between two bowls, spoon over the tagine and serve.

NUTRITION
Kcal 516 | fat 12g | sat. fat 2g | carbs 72g | sugars 17g | fibre 16g | protein 22g | salt 0.88g

KATSU AUBERGINE CURRY

This popular Japanese dish can also be made with sweet potato slices or try a mixture of both. Use panko breadcrumbs if you can as these will make the coating lovely and crunchy.

Serves 2 | Ready in 40 minutes

4 tbsp plain flour or cornflour

50g panko or dried breadcrumbs

1 aubergine, cut into 5mm-thick discs

125g basmati rice, rinsed

300g prepared vegan katsu curry sauce

BASICS
salt and black pepper, rapeseed oil

Heat the oven to 180°C/160°C fan/350°F/Gas mark 4. Place the flour or cornflour in a bowl and add 5 tablespoons of tap water or just enough to make a runny paste, then season.

Place the breadcrumbs on a plate. Dip the aubergines in the flour paste to coat on all sides, then dip into the breadcrumbs, pressing down to help the crumbs stick.

Heat a thin layer of rapeseed oil in a large frying pan over a high heat. Test it is hot enough by dropping in a few breadcrumbs, which should quickly turn golden. Reduce the heat and cook the aubergine slices in batches for 2 minutes on each side or until golden, adding a little more oil between batches. Transfer the slices to a baking tray, then cook in the oven for 15 minutes until tender.

Meanwhile, cook the rice according to the pack instructions. When the aubergine slices are ready, gently heat the curry sauce.

Divide the rice between two plates. Arrange the aubergine slices over the rice and serve with the curry sauce.

NUTRITION
Kcal 755 | fat 12g | sat. fat 1g | carbs 131g | sugars 29g | fibre 9g | protein 17g | salt 2.65g

JERK CAULIFLOWER STEAKS, RICE & BEANS

Flavoured with spice from the Caribbean, this is easy to prepare and packs a punch.

Serves 2 | Ready in 50 minutes

1 cauliflower

2 limes

2 tbsp jerk paste

100g basmati rice, rinsed

200g can red kidney beans, drained and rinsed

Cut two thick steaks from the centre of the cauliflower (you can use the rest in some of the other recipes).

In a small bowl, mix together the finely grated zest and juice of one of the limes with the jerk paste.

Brush this on both sides of the cauliflower, then place on a non-stick baking tray. Roast in the oven for about 35 to 40 minutes until tender and lightly charred.

Meanwhile, cook the rice according to the pack instructions, adding the kidney beans for the last 3 minutes, then stir in the finely grated zest of the remaining lime and juice of half the lime. Cut the other half into two wedges.

Serve the cauliflower steaks with the rice and the remaining wedges of lime to squeeze over.

NUTRITION
Kcal 356 | fat 4g | sat. fat 1g | carbs 58g | sugars 9g | fibre 11g | protein 15g | salt 0.33g

TORTILLA BOWLS

These crispy bowls can be filled with any of your favourite salad ingredients, such as cooked grains, grated carrot, beetroot, guacamole or chopped tomatoes. They also work well filled with hummus, falafel and roasted squash.

Serves 2 | Ready in 20 minutes

2 soft flour or corn tortillas

400g can mixed bean salad with corn, drained and rinsed

6 tbsp tomato salsa (hot or mild)

1 Little Gem or Baby Gem lettuce, quartered and leaves pulled apart

1 avocado, peeled, halved and stone removed, cut into strips

BASICS
rapeseed oil

Heat the oven to 180°C/160°C fan/350°F/Gas mark 4. Turn a large muffin tin upside down and brush lightly with rapeseed oil. Push a tortilla into the gaps between the muffin holes. Alternatively, lightly oil two small cake tins or ovenproof bowls and press in the tortillas.

Bake the tortillas for 5 to 7 minutes until lightly browned and crisp.

Remove from the oven and allow to cool for a few minutes.

Place the beans in a bowl and stir in 2 tablespoons of the tomato salsa. Arrange the lettuce between the two tortilla bowls, spoon over the bean mixture, then top with some slices of avocado.

Spoon over a little more salsa and serve immediately.

NUTRITION
Kcal 361 | fat 20g | sat. fat 4g | carbs 32g | sugars 8g | fibre 11g | protein 8g | salt 0.98g

SHIITAKE MUSHROOM RAMEN

Simple to make, yet so tasty. You could replace the carrots with small broccoli florets or any vegetables of your choice.

Serves 2 | Ready in 15 minutes

1 tbsp white or brown miso paste

125g shiitake mushrooms, sliced

4 spring onions, thinly sliced

1 carrot, peeled and thinly sliced

90g bundle dried ramen noodles

BASICS
vegan stock cube

Place 600ml of vegan stock and the miso paste in a medium saucepan and bring to the boil. Simmer for 2 to 3 minutes.

Add the mushrooms, most of the spring onions, reserving a few for garnish, and the carrot. Simmer for 3 to 4 minutes until just tender

Meanwhile, cook the noodles in boiling water for 3 to 4 minutes, or according to the pack instructions, until just tender. Drain and add to the soup.

Ladle the soup into two bowls and serve garnished with the reserved spring onions.

NUTRITION
Kcal 239 | fat 2g | sat. fat 0.2g | carbs 43g | sugars 8g | fibre 6g | protein 9g | salt 2.49g

MAINS

ONE PAN MUSHROOM & SPINACH PIE

A comforting one-pan pie, perfect for those cold winter nights.

Serves 2 | Ready in 30 minutes

250g mixed mushrooms, quartered

1 tbsp wholegrain mustard

3 tbsp plain vegan yoghurt

150g baby spinach, roughly chopped

4 sheets filo pastry, each halved

BASICS
olive oil, vegan stock cube, salt and black pepper

Heat the oven 180°C/160°C fan/350°F/Gas mark 4. Heat 1 tablespoon of olive oil in a non-stick ovenproof frying pan (about 20cm diameter), add the mushrooms and cook for 3 to 4 minutes.

Add 150ml of vegan stock and the wholegrain mustard and simmer until the sauce is reduced by half and thickened. Season with salt and black pepper, then stir in the yoghurt.

Add a large handful of the spinach and stir in, then remove from the heat and add the remaining spinach to make a thick layer over the top of the mushrooms.

Brush the sheets of pastry with a little oil, then crunch up the filo and arrange over the top of the spinach to cover completely. Bake in the oven for 15 minutes until the pastry is golden and crisp.

NUTRITION
Kcal 396 | fat 11g | sat. fat 1g | carbs 53g | sugars 5g | fibre 6g | protein 16g | salt 1.6g

HARISSA-ROASTED SQUASH & FREEKEH SALAD

Sweet and spicy, this warm salad is perfect for those autumnal nights.

Serves 2 | Ready in 40 minutes

½ butternut squash, unpeeled

2 tsp harissa paste

250g pouch freekeh

80g mixed baby kale or spinach

100g pomegranate seeds

BASICS
olive oil, salt and black pepper

Heat the oven to 180°C/160°C fan/350°F/Gas mark 4. Cut the butternut squash into crescents about 3cm thick, removing any seeds.

Place the squash on a baking tray, drizzle over the harissa paste and 2 teaspoons of olive oil, toss to coat in the mixture and season well. Roast in the oven for about 30 minutes until tender.

When the squash is cooked, reheat the freekeh according to the pack instructions. Tip into a bowl, add the squash and stir gently.

Divide the leaves between two plates and pile the squash and freekeh over the top. Scatter over the pomegranate seeds, drizzle with a little more oil if desired and serve immediately.

NUTRITION
Kcal 393 | fat 10g | sat. fat 1g | carbs 57g | sugars 16g | fibre 15g | protein 10g | salt 0.16g

MAINS

FALAFEL, CARROT & GRAINS BOWL

This throw-together lunch can be served hot or cold. Great for a lunch box.

Serves 2 | Ready in 20 minutes

4 falafel

1 small unwaxed lemon

250g pouch mixed grains, such as red rice, quinoa and freekeh

50g spinach

1 carrot, peeled and coarsely grated

BASICS
olive oil, salt and black pepper

If serving hot, heat the oven to 200°C/180°C fan/400°F/ Gas mark 6. Place the falafel on a baking tray and bake for 12 minutes, or according to the pack instructions, until heated through.

Meanwhile, finely grate the zest from the lemon into a bowl and cut in half. Squeeze the juice from one half, whisk together with 1 tablespoon of olive oil to make a dressing and season to taste.

Heat the grains according to the pack instructions, place in a bowl and add the spinach to wilt, then pour over the dressing and mix well. Cut the remaining lemon half into two wedges.

Spoon the dressed grains into two bowls, top with the falafel and carrot and add the lemon wedges to squeeze over.

If serving cold, just pile all the ingredients into two bowls.

NUTRITION
Kcal 377 | fat 13g | sat. fat 2g | carbs 48g | sugars 5g | fibre 10g | protein 12g | salt 0.14g

THAI RED PUMPKIN CURRY

You could use slices of courgette in place of the beans. Use any Thai curry paste for this recipe – just check it is vegan.

Serves 2 | Ready in 30 minutes

2 tbsp Thai red curry paste

400g peeled, deseeded and
 chopped pumpkin or
 butternut squash

400ml can coconut milk (use
 reduced-fat, if preferred)

100g Thai or jasmine rice, rinsed

125g green beans, cut into 5cm
 pieces

BASICS
rapeseed oil, salt
 and black pepper

Heat 1 tablespoon of rapeseed oil in a wok or pan over a medium heat, add the curry paste and cook for 2 minutes until fragrant. Stir in the pumpkin or squash and stir to coat, then cook for 2 to 3 minutes until lightly browned.

Pour in the coconut milk, bring to the boil, then reduce the heat and simmer for 15 to 20 minutes until the pumpkin or squash is just tender.

Meanwhile, cook the rice in a pan of lightly salted boiling water according to the pack instructions.

Stir the beans into the curry and cook for 3 to 4 minutes until the vegetables are tender. Season to taste.

Serve the rice in bowls and spoon over the curry.

NUTRITION (USING REDUCED-FAT COCONUT MILK)
Kcal 548 | fat 25g | sat. fat 13g | carbs 67g | sugars 13g | fibre 8g | protein 9g | salt 0.6g

SUMMER OLIVE TART

So simple to make, this is an impressive centrepiece for entertaining your friends. Serve with some mixed salad leaves.

Serves 4 | Ready in 30 minutes

1 courgette, halved widthways

1 yellow or red pepper, or mixture of both, deseeded and cut into 8 chunks

320g pack ready-rolled vegan puff pastry

4 tbsp olive tapenade

8 cherry or baby plum tomatoes

BASICS
olive oil, salt and black pepper

Heat the oven to 200°C/180°C fan/400°F/Gas mark 6. Cut the courgette lengthways into 2mm-thick strips.

Heat a griddle pan over a high heat, brush with a little olive oil, then add a few of the courgette strips and cook for 2 minutes on one side. Turn over and cook until softened. Remove to a plate and repeat with the remaining courgette strips, then the pepper chunks.

Unroll the pastry and place on a non-stick baking sheet. Using a sharp knife, score a 2.5cm rim along all sides of the rectangle, being careful not to cut all the way through.

Spread over the tapenade within the border. Add the griddled pepper and courgette, then scatter over the tomatoes. Season well with salt and black pepper.

Bake for 12 to 15 minutes until the pastry is risen and golden around the edges. Cut into quarters to serve.

NUTRITION
Kcal 386 | fat 26g | sat. fat 11g | carbs 30g | sugars 5g | fibre 4g | protein 6g | salt 1g

WARMING LENTIL PIE

Perfect for Sunday lunch accompanied by some steamed spring greens or cabbage. This pie is topped with an olive oil mash, but you could use sweet potatoes to top it, if preferred.

Serves 3 | Ready in 40 minutes

550g potatoes, peeled and chopped

1 onion, chopped

2 carrots, peeled and chopped

400g can chopped tomatoes with herbs

400g can green lentils

BASICS
olive oil, salt and black pepper, vegan milk

Heat the oven to 190°C/170°C fan/375°F/Gas mark 5. Cook the potatoes in a pan of lightly salted boiling water until tender.

Meanwhile, heat 1 tablespoon of olive oil in a medium pan. Add the onion and carrots and cook over a medium heat for 3 to 4 minutes. Stir in the chopped tomatoes and 100ml of tap water, then cover and simmer for 10 minutes. Add the can of lentils, including their juice, stir well, cover and cook for 5 minutes. Season to taste.

Drain the potatoes and mash in the pan with 3 tablespoons of olive oil and 2 tablespoons of vegan milk until smooth. Season to taste.

Transfer the lentil mixture to an ovenproof dish, then cover with the mash. Cook in the oven for 10 to 15 minutes until the potato topping is golden and the filling bubbling.

NUTRITION
Kcal 397 | fat 16g | sat. fat 2g | carbs 49g | sugars 12g | fibre 9g | protein 10g | salt 0.35g

ASPARAGUS, BASIL & LEMON RISOTTO

Spelt is an ancient member of the wheat family and has a slightly nutty flavour. You can also make this risotto with arborio rice, if you prefer. Follow the same method as below, adding a little more stock if necessary.

Serves 2 | Ready in 30 minutes

1 bunch asparagus (about 250g), woody stems removed

1 onion, chopped

125g pearled spelt, rinsed

2 tbsp chopped basil, plus extra leaves for garnish

finely grated zest and juice 1 unwaxed lemon

BASICS
vegan stock cube, olive oil, black pepper

Finely chop the asparagus stalks, leaving the tips whole. Cook the asparagus tips and stalks in a saucepan of simmering water for 3 minutes, until al dente. Drain, reserving the water. Pour this water over 1 vegan stock cube and make up to 600ml with boiling water, stirring to dissolve.

Meanwhile, heat 1 tablespoon of olive oil in a saucepan over a medium heat and cook the onion for 2 to 3 minutes until softened. Stir in the spelt and cook for 1 minute until the grains are coated in the onion mixture.

Pour in 100ml of the hot stock and cook for 2 to 3 minutes until absorbed. Gradually add the remaining hot stock, 125ml at a time and stirring constantly, until most of the liquid has been absorbed. Cook for about 15 minutes, or until most of the stock has been absorbed and the spelt is tender, but still firm.

Stir in the asparagus tips and stalks and cook for 2 to 3 minutes until heated through. Stir in the chopped basil, lemon zest and juice. Cover and stand for 1 minute. Serve in bowls with black pepper and extra basil leaves.

NUTRITION
Kcal 329 | fat 8g | sat. fat 1g | carbs 44g | sugars 10g | fibre 10g | protein 14g | salt 1.49g

SWEET POTATO GNOCCHI WITH SAGE

These light potato dumplings take a little time to prepare but are worth the effort. Serve with a mixed leaf salad. The gnocchi are also delicious tossed in a free-from pesto sauce. You can freeze the gnocchi on a tray. When frozen, transfer to a freezer bag and they can be cooked straight from the freezer.

Serves 3 | Ready in 1 hour

2 medium sweet potatoes

125g plain flour

50g vegan spread

25g pine nuts, toasted

12 sage leaves

BASICS
salt and black pepper

Heat the oven to 200°C/180°C fan/400°F/Gas mark 6. Prick the sweet potatoes all over with a fork and bake them for 40 to 45 minutes until tender.

Cut the potatoes in half and cool slightly, then scoop out the flesh into a bowl. Mash until smooth and stir in 1 teaspoon of salt and a little pepper. Gradually add the flour until you have a soft dough that is no longer sticky. Divide into two even-sized pieces and on a lightly floured surface, roll each piece into a sausage, 2.5cm wide by 20cm long. Cut each sausage into eight pieces. Press down lightly on each gnocchi with the back of a fork.

Bring a large pan of salted water to the boil, drop in half the gnocchi and wait for them to float to the top – this should take about 3 to 4 minutes. Scoop them out with a slotted spoon and place in a warm bowl. Cook the remaining gnocchi in the same way.

Heat a large frying pan and add the vegan spread, pine nuts and sage leaves and cook until the sage is crispy and the pine nuts lightly toasted. Toss in the gnocchi to coat. Serve immediately.

NUTRITION
Kcal 453 | fat 17g | sat. fat 3g | carbs 64g | sugars 17g | fibre 7g | protein 7g | salt 1.92g

PASTA THREE WAYS

No need to reach for those jars of pasta sauce with these easy recipes, which are full of flavour and perfect for a simple meal.

Serves 2 | Ready in 20 minutes

**200g dried pasta, whatever
  shape you wish**

SPINACH AND CASHEW PESTO

Store any remaining pesto in the fridge, just topping up with a little more olive oil. This recipe works well with spaghetti or linguine.

**50g baby spinach leaves or
  shredded kale leaves**

50g cashew nuts

1 garlic clove, roughly chopped

25g basil leaves

**BASICS
olive oil, salt and black pepper**

To make the pesto, place the spinach or kale, cashews, garlic and basil in a food processor and blitz until chopped. Add 4 tablespoons of olive oil and season, then blitz again until smooth.

Meanwhile, cook the pasta in a saucepan of salted boiling water according to the packet instructions until al dente. Drain well, reserving a little of the cooking water, and return to the pan to keep warm. Stir in the pesto to coat, then add a little of the reserved water to bind together.

Serve immediately with an extra grind of black pepper.

NUTRITION
Kcal 605 | fat 19g | sat. fat 3g | carbs 85g | sugars 8g | fibre 7g | protein 20g | salt 0.12g

MAINS

FRESH TOMATO SAUCE

This recipe works well with penne or rigatoni.

1 small onion, finely chopped

250g small cherry or plum tomatoes

2 tbsp sundried tomato paste

rocket leaves

BASICS
olive oil, salt and black pepper

Heat 1 tablespoon of olive oil in a large frying pan, then add the onion and cook for 2 to 3 minutes until the onion has softened. Stir in the cherry or plum tomatoes and cook for 5 to 6 minutes, stirring occasionally, until the tomatoes have softened and start to collapse. Gently squash some of them with the back of a spoon. Stir in the tomato paste and season to taste.

Meanwhile, cook the pasta in a saucepan of salted boiling water according to the packet instructions until al dente. Drain well, reserving some of the cooking water, and return to the pan to keep warm.

Pour the sauce over the drained pasta and toss well. Add a little of the reserved pasta water if needed. Serve immediately with the rocket leaves and an extra grind of black pepper.

NUTRITION
Kcal 474 | fat 8g | sat. fat 1g | carbs 81g | sugars 10g | fibre 8g | protein 16g | salt 0.1g

MAINS

PASTA THREE WAYS

LEMON & COURGETTE

This recipe works well with tagliatelle or pappardelle. If you prefer, swap the chilli for a crushed garlic clove.

2 courgettes, coarsely grated

½ red chilli, deseeded and finely chopped or a pinch dried chilli flakes

finely grated zest and juice 1 large unwaxed lemon

1 tbsp chopped mint

BASICS
olive oil, salt and black pepper

Heat 2 tablespoons of olive oil in a frying pan over a medium heat, add the courgette and chilli and cook for about 5 minutes until softened.

Meanwhile, cook the pasta in a saucepan of salted boiling water according to the packet instructions until al dente. Drain well, reserving some of the cooking water, and return to the pan to keep warm.

Add the lemon zest and juice to the courgette, then stir in the pasta and about 2 tablespoons of the reserved cooking water. Season and toss to coat. Stir in the chopped mint.

Serve in bowls with extra black pepper.

NUTRITION
Kcal 494 | fat 13g | sat. fat 2g | carbs 75g | sugars 5g | fibre 7g | protein 15g | salt 0.01g

TASTE OF THE SEA TOFU & CHIPS

You may have some batter left, in which case keep it and use for tempura vegetables – courgettes, mushrooms and cauliflower work well.

Serves 2 | Ready in 30 minutes

250g oven chips

200g firm tofu

125g pack tempura batter mix

4 x ½ nori sheets

300g can mushy peas

BASICS
salt and black pepper,
  rapeseed oil

Heat the oven to 200°C/180°C fan/400°F/Gas mark 6. Place the chips on a baking tray and cook for 25 to 30 minutes until golden, or according to the pack instructions.

Meanwhile, place the tofu between two pieces of kitchen paper and put a chopping board or heavy weight on top. Leave for at least 10 minutes, to remove excess water, then cut into four fingers.

Make up the batter mix, according to the pack instructions, with cold water.

Season the tofu, then wrap each finger in a piece of nori (the moisture in the tofu will help it stick). Dampen the edges to seal.

Heat 450ml (or enough to come halfway up the sides) of the rapeseed oil in a pan or deep-fat fryer to 180°C, or until a little bit of the batter sizzles and goes crispy. Add the tofu to the batter mix, turn to coat, then carefully place in the hot oil. Fry for 3 to 4 minutes until lightly golden.

Heat the mushy peas and serve with the tofu and chips.

NUTRITION
Kcal 733 | fat 23g | sat. fat 3g | carbs 94g | sugars 4g | fibre 13g | protein 31g | salt 1.47g

LEEK & POTATO PIE

Tender, melting potatoes and leeks with a shortcrust pastry top. If you prefer, you could use puff pastry.

Serves 2 | Ready in 40 minutes

300g potatoes, peeled and sliced

1 leek, sliced

1 tsp cornflour

1 tbsp chopped thyme or
   rosemary

250g vegan shortcrust pastry

BASICS
olive oil, vegan stock cube,
   vegan milk, salt and
   black pepper

Cook the potatoes in a pan of simmering water for 4 to 5 minutes until just tender, then drain. Meanwhile, heat 1 tablespoon of olive oil in a saucepan and gently cook the leek for 3 to 4 minutes until softened. Stir in the cornflour, then gradually stir in 150ml of vegan stock.

Add the potatoes and herbs and stir to coat. Season well, then divide the mixture between two small pie dishes or one larger dish.

Roll out the pastry and cut a thin strip of pastry to place around the edge of the dishes, pressing down with a little water to seal, then lightly brush the top of the pastry strip with more water. Place the remaining pastry over and seal again, using a fork to press the two pieces of pastry together. Trim the excess and make a hole in the centre of the pies for the steam to escape. Lightly brush all over with milk.

Bake for 25 to 30 minutes until the top is golden and the potatoes inside are tender. Serve immediately.

NUTRITION
Kcal 776 | fat 46g | sat. fat 16g | carbs 74g | sugars 4g | fibre 9g | protein 12g | salt 0.9g

MAINS

RICE NOODLE CHILLI STIR-FRY

This zingy, speedy stir-fry is perfect for when time is short. Choose a stir-fry pack with vegetables such as pak choi, tenderstem and butternut squash.

Serves 2 | Ready in 15 minutes

125g rice noodles

250g pack stir-fry vegetables

1 tbsp grated fresh ginger

4 tbsp sweet chilli sauce

finely grated zest and juice 1 lime

BASICS
rapeseed oil

Cook the noodles in a pan of boiling water according to the pack instructions. Drain and refresh under cold water and set aside.

Heat 1 tablespoon of rapeseed oil and add the vegetables.

Cook over a high heat for 2 to 3 minutes, then add the ginger and continue to stir-fry until the vegetables are tender.

In a small bowl, mix together the chilli sauce and lime juice.

Add the noodles to the pan, followed by the sauce, and toss well so everything is coated in the sauce.

Divide between two bowls, then sprinkle over the lime zest. Serve immediately.

NUTRITION
Kcal 359 | fat 5g | sat. fat 0.2g | carbs 69g | sugars 17g | fibre 3g | protein 8g | salt 1.04g

GRIDDLED PEACH & ALMOND SALAD

This fresh-tasting salad is perfect for a hot summer's day. Griddling the peaches brings out their sweetness or you could lightly char them on the edge of a barbecue.

Serves 2 | Ready in 20 minutes

25g almonds, roughly chopped

2 just ripe small peaches or nectarines, halved and stones removed, each cut into 8 wedges

200g tenderstem broccoli or pack mixed tenderstem, sugar snaps, green beans and asparagus

2 tbsp free-from basil pesto

75g mixed watercress, spinach and rocket leaves

BASICS
salt and black pepper, olive oil

Heat a griddle pan. When hot, lightly toast the almonds and transfer to a plate. Return the pan to the heat and add the peaches or nectarines. Cook for 2 minutes on each side until they have good griddle marks.

Meanwhile, cook the vegetables in a pan of lightly salted boiling water for 3 minutes, until just tender, drain and refresh under cold water.

Mix together the pesto with 1 tablespoon of olive oil and 1 tablespoon of cold water.

Arrange the leaves on a plate, add the vegetables and peach or nectarine slices, drizzle over some pesto and scatter with the almonds.

Serve immediately with a good grind of black pepper.

NUTRITION
Kcal 260 | fat 19g | sat. fat 2g | carbs 10g | sugars 8g | fibre 5g | protein 9g | salt 0.22g

NEW POTATO & FENNEL BAKE

Enjoy the flavours of the Mediterranean with this easy tray bake, which will be on the table in under 40 minutes. It will become a weekly favourite.

Serves 2 | Ready in 35 minutes

1 fennel bulb, cut into 6

250g baby new potatoes, halved lengthways

2 garlic cloves, crushed

200g cherry tomatoes

125g ciabatta with olives, torn into large chunks

BASICS
olive oil, salt and black pepper

Heat the oven to 200°C/180°C fan/400°F/Gas mark 6. Cook the fennel and potatoes in a pan of boiling water for 5 minutes. Drain and place on a baking tray.

Mix 2 tablespoons of olive oil with the garlic, drizzle over the vegetables, season well with salt and black pepper and toss to coat. Roast for 15 minutes.

Add the tomatoes and bread and toss everything together. Return to the oven and cook for a further 10 minutes, or until the potatoes and bread are golden and crisp.

Divide between two plates and serve immediately.

NUTRITION
Kcal 404 | fat 17g | sat. fat 2g | carbs 50g | sugars 8g | fibre 9g | protein 9g | salt 0.66g

CHERMOULA-SPICED BROCCOLI FRITTERS

Chermoula is a North African spice paste, flavoured with lemon, coriander, parsley, cumin and chilli. For a light meal, serve the patties with salad leaves, but they are also delicious made into burgers and served in rolls.

Serves 2 | Ready in 30 minutes

175g broccoli florets

100g couscous

2 tbsp chermoula spice paste

2 tbsp plain flour

bag mixed salad leaves

BASICS
salt and black pepper,
  rapeseed oil

Cook the broccoli in a pan of lightly salted boiling water for 4 to 5 minutes until just tender, drain and refresh under cold water. Drain well, place in a food processor and pulse until finely chopped.

Meanwhile, place the couscous in a bowl and pour over 100ml boiling water or to just cover. Cover with cling film and leave to stand for 4 to 5 minutes, until the couscous has absorbed all the water. Stir in the spice paste to coat the grains, season well and stir in the broccoli. Add the flour to bind together.

Shape the mixture into six balls and flatten into patties.

Heat 2 tablespoons of the rapeseed oil in a frying pan. Add the patties and cook over a low heat for 4 to 5 minutes on each side, until lightly golden.

Serve the patties with the salad leaves.

NUTRITION
Kcal 435 | fat 16g | sat. fat 1g | carbs 57g | sugars 3g | fibre 6g | protein 12g | salt 0.4g

Baking & Sweet Things

The first two chapters have the main meal times covered. This chapter covers everything else in between! Vegan baking is simple – and you'll find cookies, brownies, cakes, scones, breads, tarts, muffins and meringue here. And if you are after a pudding, there are plenty to choose from – including cooling ice cream to comforting rice pudding and pretty panna cotta.

What would you like?

Baking & Sweet Things

Peanut butter & chocolate
chip cookies

Salted chocolate
fudge brownies

Orange polenta cake

Sun-blushed tomato
& olive scones

Potato & rosemary focaccia

Lemon drizzle cake

Apricot & almond tart

Raspberry & apple muffins

Celebration pavlova

Rhubarb & ginger crumbles

Rice pudding with poached plums

Griddled lime & chilli pineapple

Coconut, mango & chilli ginger ice cream

Chocolate orange pots

Coconut & lime panna cotta

PEANUT BUTTER & CHOCOLATE CHIP COOKIES

These delicious cookies are chewy in the middle and crisp on the outside. Perfect with a cup of tea or coffee.

Makes 18 cookies | Ready in 30 minutes

100g vegan spread, suitable for baking

125g caster sugar

100g crunchy peanut butter

150g self-raising flour

125g dark chocolate chips

Heat the oven to 180°C/160°C fan/350°F/Gas mark 4. Line two baking sheets with baking paper.

Using a hand-held electric whisk, beat the spread and sugar together in a large bowl until pale and creamy. Whisk in the peanut butter.

Using a metal spoon, stir in the flour and chocolate chips until thoroughly mixed together.

Taking tablespoons of the dough, roll the dough into about 18 balls.

Place on the lined baking sheets, leaving space around each ball as they will expand during cooking. Flatten the balls slightly. Bake in the oven for 10 to 12 minutes or until golden.

Allow to cool on the sheets for 5 minutes, then transfer to a cooling rack.

NUTRITION (PER COOKIE)
Kcal 163 | fat 9g | sat. fat 3g | carbs 16g | sugars 9g | fibre 1g | protein 3g | salt 0.17g

BAKING & SWEET THINGS

SALTED CHOCOLATE FUDGE BROWNIES

These chocolate brownies are deliciously fudgy. If you prefer, you can omit the sea salt or try adding some chopped nuts for variation. The flaxseeds act as a binder.

Makes 16 brownies | Ready in 40 minutes

2 tbsp ground flaxseeds

150g dark chocolate chips or chocolate, broken into small pieces (70% cocoa solids)

125g vegan spread, suitable for baking

200g golden caster sugar

100g plain flour

BASICS
salt

Heat the oven to 180°C/160°C fan/350°F/Gas mark 4. Grease and line the base of an 18–20cm square cake tin with baking paper.

In a small bowl, combine the flaxseeds with 5 tablespoons of cold water, stir well and set to one side.

Melt the chocolate in a heatproof bowl over a saucepan of simmering water, stirring occasionally, or in the microwave. Remove from the heat and allow to cool slightly.

In a large mixing bowl, using a hand-held electric whisk, beat together the spread and sugar until pale and fluffy.

Whisk in the chocolate mixture and flax 'eggs' and beat until well combined, then using a metal spoon, stir in the flour and 1 teaspoon of salt.

Pour into the prepared tin, sprinkle with a little extra salt, if you like, and bake for 20 minutes until just set – the centre will still be slightly gooey. Cool in the tin for 10 minutes, then transfer to a cooling rack. When completely cold, remove the baking paper and cut into squares.

NUTRITION (PER BROWNIE, NOT INCLUDING SPRINKLED SALT)
Kcal 173 | fat 9g | sat. fat 3g | carbs 21g | sugars 15g | fibre 1g | protein 1g | salt 0.37g

ORANGE POLENTA CAKE

This cake is deliciously moist and sticky, perfect with a cup of tea. Use blood oranges when in season. You could replace the oranges with the zest and juice of 2 large unwaxed lemons, plus 1 unwaxed lemon for the syrup.

Serves 8 | Ready in 40 minutes

3 oranges

100ml agave nectar or maple syrup, plus 4 tbsp for the syrup

125g fine cornmeal (polenta)

75g ground almonds

100g self-raising flour

BASICS
olive oil, vegan milk

Heat the oven to 170°C/150°C fan/325°F/Gas mark 3. Lightly oil an 18cm or 20cm round cake tin and line the base with baking paper.

Finely grate the zest and squeeze the juice from two of the oranges. Put the juice in a jug and whisk in the nectar or syrup, 100ml of vegan milk and 100ml of olive oil.

Put the cornmeal, almonds, orange zest and flour in a bowl, stir in the wet ingredients until combined, then pour into the prepared tin.

Bake for 30 to 35 minutes or until a skewer inserted in the middle comes out clean. Leave in the tin.

Pare the zest from the remaining orange and squeeze the juice into a small pan. Add the 4 tablespoons nectar or syrup and the zest and simmer for 5 minutes.

Prick the top of the hot cake all over with a cocktail stick. Gradually pour over half the syrup. Leave for a few minutes to soak in, then repeat with the remaining syrup. Allow to cool in the tin, then turn out and serve in slices.

NUTRITION
Kcal 322 | fat 19g | sat. fat 2g | carbs 32g | sugars 10g | fibre 1g | protein 6g | salt 0.12g

BAKING & SWEET THINGS

SUN-BLUSHED TOMATO & OLIVE SCONES

Delicious served warm, split in half and smothered with vegan spread.

Makes 8 scones | Ready in 40 minutes

250g self-raising flour

50g vegan spread, suitable
  for baking

6 sun-blushed tomatoes,
  chopped

6 pitted black olives, sliced

1 tsp dried mixed herbs or 1 tbsp
  chopped basil

BASICS
salt and black pepper,
  vegan milk

Heat the oven to 200°C/180°C fan/400°F/Gas mark 6. Put the flour, a pinch of salt and a little black pepper in a bowl, then rub in the spread until the mixture resembles fine breadcrumbs.

Add the tomatoes, olives and herbs, stir, then pour in 125ml of vegan milk, a little bit at a time, stirring with a rounded knife until the mixture forms a soft dough and comes together in a ball.

Gently knead on a lightly floured surface to remove any cracks. Roll out to a 2cm thickness, then, using a 6cm round pastry cutter, cut into rounds. Gather any spare bits of dough and knead lightly, roll out and make more scones.

Place the scones on a baking tray, spacing them a little apart. Brush the tops with milk and bake for 10 to 12 minutes until risen and golden brown. Transfer to a cooling rack.

Delicious served warm or cold, split in half and spread with extra vegan spread.

NUTRITION (PER SCONE)
Kcal 162 | fat 5g | sat. fat 1g | carbs 24g | sugars 1g | fibre 1g | protein 3g | salt 0.48g

POTATO & ROSEMARY FOCACCIA

This dimpled Italian bread can be flavoured with herbs, sundried tomatoes or olives. Follow this basic recipe, adding your favourite ingredients.

Serves 8 | Ready in 50 minutes, plus 2 hours rising

350g strong white bread flour

2 tsp fast-action dried yeast

6 new potatoes

4 garlic cloves, crushed

small sprigs rosemary, roughly chopped

BASICS
olive oil, salt

Sift the flour into a large mixing bowl, add 1 teaspoon of salt and stir in the yeast. Lightly oil a 28cm x 18cm oblong cake tin about 4cm deep, and set aside.

Make a well in the centre of the flour and stir in 250ml warm water and 50ml of olive oil until the mixture starts to come together to form a smooth dough.

Transfer to a lightly oiled surface and knead for 10 minutes until smooth and elastic. Place in a clean bowl, cover with a tea towel, and leave to rise in a warm place for 1 hour or until doubled in size.

Punch the dough to remove the large air bubbles, then put on a lightly floured surface. Knead lightly, then press into the prepared tin using your fist to reach the corners and flatten out with your hand.

Cover loosely with oiled cling film and leave to rise for about 40 minutes to 1 hour or until the dough has risen to the top of the tin.

Meanwhile, boil the potatoes in a pan of lightly salted water for 10 to 15 minutes until tender. Drain and allow to cool slightly, then cut into thin slices.

Mix 2 tablespoons of olive oil in a small bowl with the crushed garlic and rosemary and leave to one side

Heat the oven to 200°C/180°C fan/400°F/Gas mark 6. Using your fingertips, make dimples all over the surface of the dough, then drizzle over some of the garlic and rosemary oil. Scatter over the sliced potato.

Drizzle with the remaining oil, then sprinkle with course salt. Bake for 20 to 25 minutes until risen and golden. Delicious served warm.

NUTRITION (NOT INCLUDING SPRINKLED SALT)
Kcal 268 | fat 10g | sat. fat 1g | carbs 38g | sugars 1g | fibre 2g | protein 7g | salt 0.62g

LEMON DRIZZLE CAKE

This cake is deliciously lemony and moist. It will keep in an airtight container for 3 to 4 days.

Makes 10 slices | Ready in 1 hour

100g ground almonds

150g self-raising flour

1 tsp baking powder

225g caster sugar

finely grated zest and juice 2
   large unwaxed lemons

BASICS

rapeseed oil, vegan milk
   (almond works well)

Heat the oven to 180°C/160°C fan/350°F/Gas mark 4. Lightly oil a 900g loaf tin and line the base with baking paper.

In a large bowl, mix together the almonds, flour, baking powder, 150g of the sugar and the lemon zest.

Add 100ml of rapeseed oil, 150ml of vegan milk and half the lemon juice; stir well until combined. Pour into the prepared tin and bake for 30 to 35 minutes until golden brown and a skewer inserted into the middle comes out clean.

Remove from the oven and prick the top of the cake all over with a cocktail stick about 20 times.

While the cake is cooking, put the remaining caster sugar in a bowl and stir in the remaining lemon juice. Leave to one side. Drizzle over the hot cake, slowly, waiting a few moments before adding more so that it all soaks in. It will leave a crust on the cake as the juices soak in.

Cool in the tin for 10 minutes, then remove from the tin and transfer to a cooling rack. When cool, serve in slices.

NUTRITION
Kcal 301 | fat 16g | sat. fat 1g | carbs 35g | sugars 23g | fibre 1g | protein 4g | salt 0.27g

APRICOT & ALMOND TART

Apricots and almonds are a perfect combination. This dessert is so easy to make and sure to impress your friends.

Serves 8 | Ready in 30 minutes

320g pack ready-rolled vegan puff pastry

6 tbsp apricot jam

25g ground almonds

6–8 apricots, halved and stones removed

vegan custard or ice cream

Heat the oven to 200°C/180°C fan/400°F/Gas mark 6. Unroll the pastry and place on a non-stick baking sheet. Using a sharp knife, score a 2.5cm rim along the sides of the rectangle, being careful not to cut all the way through.

Spread 4 tablespoons of the jam on the base within the marked edges. Spoon the almonds over the pastry, then top with the apricots, cut-side up.

Bake for 20 minutes, until the pastry is risen and golden. Warm the remaining apricot jam in a small pan or in the microwave, then brush over the apricots. Serve in slices, with vegan custard or ice cream.

NUTRITION (EXCLUDING CUSTARD)
Kcal 218 | fat 12g | sat. fat 5g | carbs 22g | sugars 10g | fibre 2g | protein 3g | salt 0.35g

RASPBERRY & APPLE MUFFINS

Deliciously moist, these make a great mid-morning or afternoon treat.

Makes 12 muffins | Ready in 40 minutes

275g self-raising flour

2 tsp baking powder

125g caster sugar

1 eating apple, cored and coarsely grated

200g raspberries

BASICS
vegan milk, rapeseed oil

Heat the oven to 190°C/170°C fan/375°F/Gas mark 5. Line a muffin tin with 12 paper muffin cases.

Sift the flour and baking powder into a large mixing bowl. Stir in the caster sugar.

In a jug, whisk together 250ml of vegan milk and 90ml of rapeseed oil with a fork. Pour over the dry ingredients and stir until just combined. Gently fold in the apple and raspberries.

Spoon into the cases and cook in the centre of the oven for 20 to 25 minutes until well risen and golden. Leave to cool for a few minutes, then transfer to a cooling rack.

Delicious served warm or cold.

NUTRITION (PER MUFFIN)
Kcal 208 | fat 8g | sat. fat 1g | carbs 29g | sugars 12g | fibre 2g | protein 3g | salt 0.4g

BAKING & SWEET THINGS

CELEBRATION PAVLOVA

If you prefer, you can make 6 individual meringue nests rather than one large pavlova. You could also add a little bit of food colouring to create a ripple effect, or flavour with vanilla extract.

Serves 6 | Ready in 4 hours

- **400g can chickpeas, chilled for 1 hour**
- **½ tsp cream of tartar**
- **125g icing sugar (for cream)**
- **200ml can coconut cream, chilled**
- **200g mixed tropical fruit, mixed berries or your favourite fruit**

Heat the oven to 110°C/90°C fan/225°F/Gas mark ¼. Line a baking tray with baking paper.

Drain the chilled chickpea liquid into a bowl (save the chickpeas to make hummus or use in a salad or tagine). Whisk the liquid on high speed using the whisk attachment on a stand mixer or using a hand-held electric whisk. Beat for around 10 minutes until white and fluffy. It should have doubled in volume and stand in soft peaks.

Add the cream of tartar, whisk for 1 minute, then gradually whisk in the icing sugar, 1 tablespoon at a time, fully incorporating each tablespoon before adding the next. The mixture will be stiff and glossy.

Spoon the mixture onto the lined baking tray in a large circle. Bake in the oven for 2 hours, then turn off the oven and allow to cool in the oven for at least 1 hour.

Beat the coconut cream in a bowl with a hand-held electric whisk for about 4 minutes until thickened, adding a little extra icing sugar to taste. Spoon over the meringue and top with the fruit. Serve immediately.

NUTRITION
Kcal 227 | fat 12g | sat. fat 10g | carbs 28g | sugars 26g | fibre 1g | protein 2g | salt 0.01g

BAKING & SWEET THINGS

RHUBARB & GINGER CRUMBLES

Rhubarb and ginger is a perfect combination, just right for a Sunday treat served with lashings of vegan custard.

Serves 2 | Ready in 40 minutes

350g rhubarb, cut into 2.5cm pieces

2 pieces preserved stem ginger, finely chopped, and 5 tbsp ginger syrup

2 tbsp vegan spread, suitable for baking

150g oats (instant oats work well)

300ml vegan custard

Heat the oven to 180°C/160°C fan/350°F/Gas mark 4. Mix together the rhubarb with the stem ginger and 3 tablespoons of the ginger syrup. Divide between two ovenproof dishes or one larger one.

To make the topping, put the remaining ginger syrup and vegan spread in a small pan and stir over a low heat until melted. Stir in the oats. Spoon over the rhubarb to cover and cook in the oven for 20–25 minutes until bubbling.

Heat the custard according to the pack instructions. Pour over the crumbles and serve.

NUTRITION
Kcal 674 | fat 18g | sat. fat 3g | carbs 109g | sugars 54g | fibre 10g | protein 15g | salt 0.35g

RICE PUDDING WITH POACHED PLUMS

This stove-top creamy vanilla pudding is so simple and quick to make. You can use any fruit, such as apples, pears or summer fruits, for the compote. When friends pop over, just double the recipe.

Serves 2 | Ready in 30 minutes

50g short-grain pudding rice, rinsed

4 tbsp caster sugar

1 tsp vanilla extract

½ tsp ground cinnamon

2 ripe plums, quartered and stoned

BASICS
vegan milk

Place the rice, 450ml of vegan milk, 2 tablespoons of the sugar and the vanilla extract in a non-stick saucepan, bring to the boil over a medium heat and simmer, uncovered, for 16 to 18 minutes, stirring frequently, until the rice is tender and sauce thickened.

Meanwhile, place the remaining sugar, 4 tablespoons of cold water, the cinnamon and plums in a separate saucepan. Bring to a gentle simmer and cook for 5 minutes or until the plums have softened, but still hold their shape.

When the rice is tender, divide the pudding between two serving dishes and top with the plum compote. Serve immediately.

NUTRITION
Kcal 342 | fat 4g | sat. fat 1g | carbs 66g | sugars 45g | fibre 3g | protein 8g | salt 0.01g

BAKING & SWEET THINGS

GRIDDLED LIME & CHILLI PINEAPPLE

Deliciously sweet pineapple fingers served in a zingy lime and chilli sauce.

Serves 2 | Ready in 10 minutes

½ red chilli, deseeded and thinly sliced

finely grated zest and juice 1 lime

50g golden or caster sugar

¼ teaspoon ground cardamom

6 fresh pineapple fingers

To make the chilli syrup, place all the ingredients except the pineapple in a small pan with 75ml of cold water, place over a low heat and stir until the sugar has dissolved. Bring to the boil, then simmer for 6 to 8 minutes until syrupy.

Meanwhile, heat a griddle pan or barbecue. When hot, add the pineapple fingers and cook for 3 to 4 minutes on each side.

Transfer to a serving plate and serve with the warm chilli syrup drizzled over the top.

NUTRITION
Kcal 120 | fat 0.1g | sat. fat 0g | carbs 29g | sugars 29g | fibre 1g | protein 0.2g | salt 0.01g

BAKING & SWEET THINGS

COCONUT, MANGO & CHILLI GINGER ICE CREAM

Simple to make and so delicious – serve on its own or with extra fruit, such as pineapple slices or peach halves, quickly seared on a griddle.

Serves 4 | Ready in 3¼ hours

400ml can coconut milk

finely grated zest and juice
   1 lime

2 stalks lemon grass, chopped

2.5cm piece fresh ginger, peeled
   and finely grated or 1 teaspoon
   ground ginger

400g frozen mango cubes

BASICS
vegan milk (coconut is good)

Place the coconut milk, 200ml of vegan milk, the lime zest and juice, lemon grass and the ginger in a saucepan. Bring to the boil, then remove from the heat and leave to infuse for 2 hours.

Strain through a sieve into a food processor, pressing with the back of a spoon, then add the frozen mango.

Blend until smooth, then transfer to a freezerproof container. Put in the freezer and freeze for 1 hour or until frozen.

Remove from the freezer for 10 minutes before you wish to serve the ice cream. Serve in scoops.

NUTRITION
Kcal 324 | fat 25g | sat. fat 22g | carbs 19g | sugars 14g | fibre 3g | protein 3g | salt 0.03g

CHOCOLATE ORANGE POTS

So easy to make and so perfect for a midweek treat, these little pots are best eaten freshly prepared. If making in advance, remove from the fridge 30 minutes before serving to allow the chocolate to soften.

Serves 2 | Ready in 20 minutes

1 orange

125g dark chocolate flavoured with orange, broken into small pieces

1 ripe avocado

2 tsp maple syrup

small handful chopped pistachios or almonds

BASICS
vegan milk (soya is good)

Finely grate the zest from the orange and place in a heatproof bowl with the chocolate. Melt over a pan of simmering water or in the microwave, stirring from time to time. Leave to one side.

Meanwhile, halve the avocado and remove the stone. Using a spoon, scoop the flesh into a food processor and blend until smooth, scraping down the sides from time to time.

Halve the orange and squeeze one half. Add 1 tablespoon of the orange juice, 1 tablespoon of vegan milk and the maple syrup, to the avocado and blend. Add the melted chocolate and blend once more until all combined.

Divide the mixture between two ramekins or small cups and chill for about 10 minutes.

Cut the remaining orange half into small pieces. Decorate the chocolate pots with some orange pieces and a small handful of chopped nuts. Serve immediately.

NUTRITION
Kcal 616 | fat 47g | sat. fat 19g | carbs 34g | sugars 24g | fibre 12g | protein 9g | salt 0.05g

COCONUT & LIME PANNA COTTA

You can buy agar agar in some supermarkets or you will find it in health food shops.

Serves 4 | Ready in about 2 hours

400ml can coconut milk

3 tbsp caster sugar

finely grated zest and juice
  2 limes

1 tsp agar agar powder

toasted coconut flakes (optional)

BASICS
vegan milk (coconut is good)

Put the coconut milk, 150ml of vegan milk, the sugar and lime juice in a pan and sprinkle over the agar agar powder. Put over a medium heat and whisk continuously until the mixture comes to the boil.

Boil for 5 minutes, whisking from time to time. Remove from the heat and stir in most of the lime zest, reserving a little for decoration.

Transfer the mixture to a measuring jug and divide among four x 150ml ramekins or moulds. Chill in the fridge for 2 hours, then turn out and serve decorated with toasted coconut flakes and extra lime zest, if you like.

NUTRITION (EXCLUDING TOASTED COCONUT FLAKES)
Kcal 244 | fat 17g | sat. fat 15g | carbs 18g | sugars 17g | fibre 1g | protein 2g | salt 0g

Index

10 9 8 7 6 5 4 3 2 1

Published in 2018 by Ebury Press an imprint of Ebury Publishing,
20 Vauxhall Bridge Road,
London SW1V 2SA

Ebury Press is part of the Penguin Random House group of companies
whose addresses can be found at global.penguinrandomhouse.com

Words by Denise Smart © Ebury Press 2018
Photography © William Shaw 2018

First published by Ebury Press in 2018

www.penguin.co.uk

A CIP catalogue record for this book is available from the British Library

ISBN 9781529103229

Designed by Maru Studio
Nutritional Consultant: Kerry Torrens

Printed and bound by Firmengruppe APPL, aprinta druck,
Wemding, Germany

Penguin Random House is committed to a sustainable future for our
business, our readers and our planet. This book is made from Forest
Stewardship Council® certified paper.